Bernese Mountain Dog Training

Dog training for your Bernese Mountain Dog puppy

©2019, Claudia Kaiser

Published by Expertengruppe Verlag

Bernese Mountain Dog Training

Dog training for your Bernese
Mountain Dog puppy

Published by Expertengruppe Verlag

Contents

About the Author

Claudia Kaiser lives with her husband and dogs Danny (2 years old) and Daika (8 years old), in an old farmhouse in beautiful Rhineland, Germany.

At first only as a dog owner, but later and after 20 years actively training dogs, she has gained a lot of experience, helping other people to train their Bernese Mountain Dog. She formed the idea of writing this book in order to reach more people, than she could have in the local dog training schools and the small circle of dog owners to whom she gave personal coaching.

The publishing of this guide book is the fruit of considerable research, writing and editing. It is designed to be a guide for all budding Bernese Mountain Dog owners, to help them get the difficult task of training right the first time, and to avoid those mistakes, which Claudia herself made at the beginning. She worked through her own bad experiences over the years, so that the reader does not have to.

Those who follow the tips and tricks covered in this guidebook are sure to have many years of pleasure from these unusual and wonderful companions.

Preface

Congratulations, you have made the excellent choice of welcoming a Bernese Mountain Dog puppy into your life. You have also chosen to buy this guidebook. This way, you have already made two good decisions.

A puppy is a small bundle of energy. His clumsiness, fluffy fur and endless trust in you, his owner, will make everyone's hearts melt. This little Bernese Mountain Dog will fulfil all your days and soon you will not be able to imagine life without him.

Before you read the next pages, you should know what to expect. This guidebook will not change your little treasure into a well-behaved dog overnight. The guide does not show you any shortcuts to success. Most importantly, reading this book alone will not change anything. Your success depends solely on you.

This guidebook will give you the necessary tools, not only to find your friend for life but also how to bring up a fear-free, happy and dependable Bernese Mountain Dog. This book is based on a gentle method of training but it also requires adherence to strict rules and needs lots of patience. It will not always be easy to stick to the rules, particularly when you see his big, trusting dog eyes looking at you. But I guarantee, that it is worth it in the long run. Not only will you be rewarded for your work, but your Bernese Mountain Dog will benefit even more.

Are you ready to invest a lot of time and love in your Bernese Mountain Dog, not only during the first weeks, but also his whole life long?

Then you have made the right choice and you can read the following pages!

From my heart, I wish you both much success and good luck.

What you need to know about your Bernese Mountain Dog

The Bernese Mountain Dog is a very special breed of dog, which is very different from many others. Training dogs involves many elements, which are the same for all breeds. However, every breed has its particular characteristics and traits which makes it unique. It is exactly these characteristics which are important in the training process.

If you want to get the best out of your Bernese Mountain Dog training, it is important that you do not just give him a general training programme but one which is especially tailored for him. Some of these methods are much more important for your Bernese Mountain Dog than, for example, a Chihuahua. It is these training modules that I will show you in the next few pages. But firstly, it is important that you get to know your dog's characteristics very well.

As the name suggests, the breed originates from the Swiss Canton of Bern, where the Bernese Mountain Dog has been serving as a herding, guarding and farm dog for more than 2000 years. However, it is little known that this breed nearly became extinct towards the end of the 19th Century and is only here now due to the efforts of a committed breed lover and his rescue programme.

It would really have been a shame to have lost this friendly, loyal and extremely attentive breed. Today, the Bernese, with his height at the withers of 2 ft and at a weight of up to 110 lb, is a good natured and well-balanced dog.

These characteristics make him predestined to be a family dog. His bonding with his "person of trust" is very strong and can sometimes become very affectionate. Tight bonding to his family and his inclusion in family life are unbelievably important for the Bernese Mountain Dog. This breed is not suited to being kept in a cage, nor to having to wait 8 hours until his master or mistress comes home from work.

If you decide to get a Bernese Mountain dog, you should be quite clear about those things. Make sure that your dog is not alone most of the time but always in company. The Berner gets along very well with other pets after, of course, a good period of familiarisation.

This dog can become quite big and therefore quite heavy and, at puppy age, grows very quickly, so it is important to take that into account if you have very small children or older people in the house. Your young, energetic four-legged friend is not always able to assess his strength and his size, which can lead to small accidents. Also, the strong herding instinct of this breed can lead to problems for small children.

As your Berner has been bred for centuries as a working dog, he needs a lot of exercise. If you want to keep him as a family dog, i.e. without his own work, it is very important that he gets enough exercise. Because of his sheer size, it is not recommended that he is kept in a very small apartment unless it has enough free space to move around.

Historically, your Bernese Mountain Dog is well suited as a hauling dog. His attentive and adaptive character also makes him a good companion. Even though he loves exercise, he is not particularly suited to sporting activities which require agility and mobility because of his bulky build.

On average a Berner will live to be 8 years old. If he is well kept, has plenty of exercise and good food, he can live up to 12 years.

You will seldomly find this dog behaving aggressively or have a hunter's instinct. As with most breeds, it is particularly important by male dogs to train them with consistency. A

Bernese Mountain Dog is mostly friendly and confident with strangers, but will probably keep his distance.

There is one thing I would like to tell you before you decide to get a Bernese Mountain Dog. If you like a clean living area and clean clothes, this is the wrong dog for you. Your home will be flooded with dog hair every day and your clothes and furniture will be full of hairs and spots of saliva from your new companion. That is a fact which I do not want to keep from you. If this does not fit with your lifestyle, perhaps a Labrador Retriever would be a better breed for you.

If you have not yet chosen your Bernese Mountain Dog, but are only thinking about buying one, I would like to give you the following tip:

It is important to buy him from a reputable breeder and inform yourself about him and his parents. Your Bernese Mountain Dog will live 9 to 13 years and therefore, it is important that he is healthy and will not have a difficult life from birth onwards because of over-breeding. Look too, at how the breeder treats his own dogs – A red light should be blinking if he keeps them in kennels – and check whether his methods are compatible with those you will be reading about in this book. If a dog has been traumatised by his breeder in early life, it takes an enormous amount of re-programming to correct it, which is too much for most dog owners.

So have a good look at the puppies, their parents and the breeder before you buy one so that you can avoid problems and ensure that you have a long and happy life with your Bernese Mountain Dog.

Cornerstones of training puppies

There are a number of books about training puppies and even more opinions. Almost every dog owner does it differently and you have probably heard a lot of tips from your friends. It would not be unusual for you to wonder, if all this training stuff really needs to be taken so seriously.

The answer to this question is a definite „YES"!

You probably do not live like a hermit. You live in a village or town, which automatically restricts the freedom of your dog. In addition, there are a lot of distractions which can affect him in today's world.

He will come into contact with other dogs, with people and children. You may take him with you when shopping, going into restaurants or while on holiday. You will receive guests and perhaps sometimes leave him alone.

It is important that your Bernese Mountain Dog is reliable in all those situations. He has to deal with his environment. He should not be afraid of noise, people or new things. He may not react aggressively and must rely completely on you as the leader of the pack.

If he has received good training from you, both of your lives will clearly be more pleasant and relaxed. Your dog will be less stressed and will be able to enjoy more freedom. For example, you can allow your Bernese Mountain Dog to run without a lead because you know that you can call him back to you at any time. And you will leave your house with a better feeling, without being afraid of what he will get up to this time.

And one more advantage: You will reduce prejudice against badly trained or malicious Bernese Mountain Dogs and help to promote a better image of owner and dog.

What must your Bernese Mountain Dog learn?

Most dog owners believe that it is enough if their dog comes to them when they call and if he does not pull on the lead. Those are two very important lessons, but they are not enough by themselves. And, more importantly, calling him back is one of the most demanding exercises of them all. That does not mean that your Bernese Mountain Dog only needs to run to you if you hold a treat to his nose. You have not mastered calling back until your dog comes to you without complaint when you call him, even while playing with other dogs. In other words, he must leave even the most distracting diversion immediately when you call him. Then you have mastered the call back.

Perhaps you will be laughed at by other dog owners but "a little" obedience is not enough. If you do not make any demands on your dog in every day life and more or less let him do what he wants, why should he obey you under other circumstances, in particular, when he is playing with other dogs, can smell something interesting or just can not be bothered?

It is important that you understand the character of your dog before you begin with puppy training. Particularly with regard to the Bernese Mountain Dog, you can barely see that they are descended from the wolf, but they are; and wolves live in packs. Despite centuries of breeding, Bernese Mountain Dogs still maintain their primitive instincts.

That means for you: In a pack there is a clear structure and a defined pecking order. At the head is the pack leader, who has a lot of self-confidence, is willing to take responsibility and always knows what he wants. He maintains discipline and does not accept subordination, not only sometimes, but ever.

If your Bernese Mountain Dog has the feeling that you are not up to this role, he will take it over. Unfortunately, he can not properly assess many dangerous situations, which can put him in danger. As an example, not recognising the danger of oncoming traffic or the long-term effects of eating human food on his body. But you can. That is why it is imperative, that you take the role of the pack leader, even if it is difficult and people may make fun of you.

The good news is: The basic training, which your Bernese Mountain Dog, being an average family dog, must take to heart, is limited. The methods you need are not rocket science and can be mastered by anyone, who has the will to do so.

The Basics

In addition to the necessary basic commands of calling back and going back on the lead, here are four more:

Your dog must sit and lie down on command. As an extension, he must be able to do both of these at a distance, even if he cannot see you. He should only move when you allow it. Lastly, your dog should be able to be left alone for a few hours without causing chaos or barking loudly.

He should be capable of carrying out all these commands, not only within your own four walls, but also outside and despite diversions from other people, dogs, loud noises or enticing smells.

If your Bernese Mountain Dog is also capable of not begging at the table or otherwise for food, not jumping up at people and not chewing things, which do not belong to him, you are both making good progress.

How do you achieve that?

Do not worry, you will not have to incessantly punish your dog. This is no longer a part of modern and effective dog training. The training in this guidebook spans two pillars:

Operant and classical conditioning.

Operant conditioning only means that your Bernese Mountain Dog would prefer to behave in a way for which he receives gratification. At the same time, he would avoid behaviour with which he associates unpleasantness. For example, if he receives a treat when he sits, he associates this with a positive feeling. If he hears a loud, shocking noise while he is contemplating eating your sandwich, he is most likely to avoid that situation next time.

As a conclusion, you will learn, on the following pages, how you can help your dog associate required positive behaviour compared to undesirable negative behaviour. This should of course be done without rebuke and should be based on consequential actions and correct linkage.

On the other hand, there is the classical conditioning with respect to the ability of your Bernese Mountain Dog to learn by himself. He will watch you and notice those things, which always happen the same way. If he recognises them, he will behave in a certain way. For example, if you always wear the same pair of shoes while taking him for a walk, in time he will not only be happy when you both walk out the door, but already when you put on the shoes.

Classical conditioning shows how important certain rituals and structures are. In this way alone, if you repeat them often enough, it will activate behavioural patterns in your dog.

Conclusion

It is not enough to demand obedience sometimes and sometimes not. In order for you and your dog to live happily together, it is necessary for your dog to obey you in all matters. You need to understand his nature and consciously behave as a masterful pack leader.

You will reward good behaviour and use negative links to counter bad behaviour. Using regular rituals, you will enable your Bernese Mountain Dog to recognise patterns and behave accordingly.

It is important to be consistent, to systemise your lessons, to practice regularly, make constant repetitions and recognise immediately linked behaviour.

Before the puppy arrives

The preparation begins even before your little Bernese Mountain Dog arrives. Part of the preparation is to read thoroughly through this guidebook, possibly more than once. After that, you need to make a few decisions in order to lay the groundwork for your relationship. These are as follows:

The main relationship

The first point to be clear about is who will take the part of the main relationship (the pack leader) for this small animal. The task is high on responsibility, will be time-consuming and will be a challenge. For this reason, it should not be given to a child. Even if it is well-meant, it would not be in the best interests of your Bernese Mountain Dog. Puppies recognise children more as friends and playmates, but not as pack leaders on whom they can orientate themselves.

The job of the pack leader is not only to assume responsibility for the training of the puppy. The main part of his responsibility is to be masterful and authoritative. The pack leader is responsible for recognising danger well in advance, to ensure all the rules are followed and to project security. In addition, the pack leader is responsible for feeding and taking care of the pack.

Arguably, one of the most difficult exercises is to ensure, that not all demands for action come from your Bernese Mountain Dog. For example demands for petting or play. No pack leader would react to such a demand. Even if you would like to, you should not react to it. In a pack, the pack leader decides what is to be done. Most dog-owners unconsciously react almost automatically, when their pet asks to be petted.

As the pack leader, it is important that you are constantly checking your behaviour towards your Bernese Mountain Dog. As in all things, small errors tend to creep in.

Privileges

Once the pack leader has been elected, the next step is to decide on privileges. You should decide, prior to your puppy arriving, how you want to structure your relationship with him. This includes what he is allowed to do and what not.

This part is particularly important, if you are not naturally authoritative or are already afraid of your position as pack leader. If that is the case, you need to carefully consider, which privileges are suitable to show him indirectly which rank he has.

Many dog owners do not care about whether their dog eats first or is allowed on the couch or bed. But all these are privileges, which are normally only allowed for the pack leader. Some people may laugh and not understand, but it is more than helpful, when your Bernese Mountain Dog is only allowed to eat after everyone else is finished. The raised sleeping places are taboo for him, because this is only allowed for the pack leader.

In addition, it is helpful to define rooms, which your Bernese Mountain Dog is now allowed to enter. This could, for example, be the kitchen, bathroom and/or the bedrooms.

You may think these rules are hard, but remember, your dog is not human and he does not think like a human. You send him contradictory signals, if you command obedience one moment and in the next moment allow him to sleep in the pack leader's place, or give him the honour of eating first.

If you send contradictory signals, your Bernese Mountain Dog will feel insecure. He will start to do what he thinks is right, because he does not have anyone whom he can rely on to guide him. The more he has success, the stronger his behaviour through operant conditioning will be.

Important by privileges and all other rules: They have to be carried out consistently by all family members and any visitors.

The time factor

As the third and last point, you must decide how much time you are willing to invest in your new life partner. Most dog owners underestimate the amount of time necessary to train their puppy, which can lead to bad behaviour later on by their dogs.

So that this does not happen, you should be clear, that good puppy training takes time, lots of time. During the first weeks and months, your little Bernese Mountain Dog will not be able to spend much time alone. He will probably need to be let out to relieve himself every two hours. Someone must consistently take care, what he is doing, so that he does not pick up any bad habits.

The first weeks are the most important for you and your puppy, so you need to allocate time, a lot of time for him. If you are working, take a few weeks off. What he does not learn early, he will never learn. Whatever you do not teach him at the beginning, it will be more difficult for him to learn later on.

The first few weeks

Getting your puppy to understand you

In order for your training to be successful from the very first day, it is important that your Bernese Mountain Dog and you speak the same language. Your little dog does not hear what you say, but listens to your voice and watches your body language. For this reason, both should be sending out the right signals. You will learn how to do this now!

Really, it is quite simple: If you want your dog to take notice of you, speak to him with an exciting and happy voice. At the same time, move in a determined and inviting manner. If you want your dog to be quieter, then speak more quietly with him and move more slowly and quietly.

The timing is just as important as the voice and the body language. Despite the beliefs of many dog owners, your Bernese Mountain Dog will never be able to understand the words you are saying. He makes his own assumptions listening to your voice, watching your body language and in the context of what has happened before.

This means for you: If you want to praise your dog, do it immediately, if he has displayed the required behaviour. The same applies, of course, to negative behaviour. How does that look in practice?

Let us assume that your little puppy has done something wrong and has chewed a shoe. You see it and, incensed, you call him to you. The puppy comes running to you and receives an angry tirade from you, that it is not correct behaviour to chew shoes. What does the puppy learn from this? He learns, that when he runs to you, he will be met with anger. This means that the next time you call him, he will think twice before coming to you. He does not understand the angry words you say to him but he has learned, that you are angry when he comes to you.

The opposite is also true. Your little puppy sits down like a good boy and you want to praise him. But directly after he sits down, he stands up again, after which you give him a treat. How does your puppy link that together? He does not link the treat with sitting down.

Always take care when you praise or rebuke him. This applies naturally not only to puppies but also for your adult Bernese Mountain Dog.

A small tip: Always take the treats you give him for training from his main meal. In addition it is recommended that you train with him when he is hungry enough to willingly take part in the exercises. Last but not least, do not get used to feeding him treats for no reason. Your Bernese Mountain Dog should know from the start that he has to work for them.

Getting him used to his new surroundings

The time has come. At last you can collect your Bernese Mountain Dog from the breeder. It is recommended that you take at least **one more person with you**. This way you can have someone drive the car, for example, while you can look after your new puppy in peace. In addition, you should be well prepared from the start. Take a collar, lead, blanket and perhaps some kitchen paper with you. It is possible, that your little Bernese Mountain Dog may feel sick.

Depending how long the journey takes, you may need to **take water** with you and after an hour, at the longest, **take a break,** so that he can relieve himself. It would be best if you can arrange to arrive home not too late. This way your Bernese Mountain Dog has time to have a good look around the house before he has to spend the first night of his life without his siblings and mother.

My **insider tip** would be, to take his blanket to the breeder a few weeks before you pick your puppy up and ask him, if he would lay the blanket out in the puppy area. This has the immense advantage that your little Bernese Mountain Dog recognises something familiar and which smells of his family. He will feel much more settled, especially at night.

Once he is home, let your little Bernese Mountain Dog out in the fresh air, either in your own garden or on a field close to your home. Be careful how you choose this place, because many dogs tend to relieve themselves in the same place, so you will be setting the foundation by showing him a "good place". This should not be a place where you like to sit or which the family uses.

After that, go back to your house or apartment. In the first few weeks, it is especially important that your puppy has a **peaceful start** so protect him from too much action. Relatives and friends are also excited about your new family member, but the needs of your four-legged friend are your priority. Allow him to explore his new surroundings intensively for a few days, before you subject him to new stimuli and impressions. There is plenty of time to introduce him to others.

Show him his new home. Show him where to find his food bowl, his blanket – or his personal space – and where his toys are. Watch how he reacts because every dog reacts differently in this very new situation.

Is he tired and does he want to find a quiet space? Is he hungry or thirsty? Perhaps you have a very bold one, who is ready to play. Try to go with his needs and do not pressurise him to do anything. During this introduction period you can check if everything is **"dog proof"** because your puppy will show you within the first few days, if he can reach wires, whether the garden fence has holes in it, or if there are any tempting plants around.

The settling in phase, during the first few weeks, is enough training for your puppy. The only thing you need to practice with him is **getting used to his name**. A lot of people underestimate something, which seems so simple. Your dog does not know, what his name is and does not understand, that some of the sounds, that you make, are meant for him. What he does know is the operant conditioning, which we discussed in the previous chapters.

After you have chosen the right name for him (this should not be too long but clear to pronounce), the conditioning begins. Always say his name in a friendly and happy tone and link it to something positive, for example a stroke. Or you can call his name and show him something interesting, like a toy. This is how your little Bernese Mountain Dog learns his name without any difficulty and he always links his name to something positive.

Do not make the mistake of using his name without reason and chat unnecessarily much to him. In that way, he loses his grasp of it and you will wonder, why your Bernese Mountain Dog does not react anymore.

Take Notice: The name of your Bernese Mountain Dog should only be used sparingly and only linked to something positive. This applies for the whole of his life.

Even more importantly than the unnecessary chatting, beware of negative links. Never reprimand your dog using his name, because he will link his name to something negative. Never shout his name to stop him from doing something. The word for that in puppy training is "no". If you do not avoid that, your Bernese Mountain Dog will tend to avoid you automatically, when you call his name. You do not want that, do you?

Building a relationship

I already mentioned at the beginning of this book, how important the pack leader is for your puppy. But how do you become this person? It is not enough just to say it. In order to build the bond, you will need to spend as much time as you can with your puppy. He needs to relate to you, respect you and trust you.

The most proven method to strengthen your bond is to take **bonding walks**. These are carried out only by the pack leader and should not be longer than 5 to 15 minutes in the first 16 weeks. At the beginning it will be enough to take him on one bonding walk per day because you will not want to flood his senses.

The good thing about these walks is, that you can utilise the **following instinct** of your four-legged friend, which is strongest during the first few weeks. A puppy knows instinctively, that he cannot survive alone and because of that, he looks for a protective bond. If you continue with these walks determinedly, he will automatically and intensively learn that he must always be attentive to you.

What does a bonding walk look like at its best?

Take your puppy out into the country. Find a quiet field where your little Bernese Mountain Dog will not be distracted by other dogs, people, or cars. He should concentrate completely on you. Take him and put him in the middle of the field. Then start walking. Not quickly, but also not too slowly. If your Bernese Mountain Dog is a little shy, you can encourage him by saying a few happy-sounding words, but please, nothing more.

You will see, he will follow you instinctively. Make sure that he has to try hard to keep up with you and change direction every few yards. Take notice of your own body language. It should show determination and you must not hesitate. Should your puppy walk past you and not take notice of you, you must show him, that this behaviour has consequences. Immediately, change direction, do a 180° turn and walk quickly without hesitation.

Because of his follower instinct, your puppy will start to follow you after a few seconds. As with all exercises, the most important thing is, that you carry them out with consistency. Practise once a day for between 5 and 15 minutes and take notice, of what your puppy is doing. If he is not taking notice of you, then ensure that he does by pursuing the direction change training. When you are finished with the training, pick him up and carry him back to the car.

In addition to the bonding walks, **exploratory walks** are also good for your Bernese Mountain Dog. Puppies are naturally inquisitive and Bernese Mountain Dogs particularly so. Integrate a small nature adventure into your routine. Not only does this improve his motoric skills, but also it will satisfy his innate inquisitiveness.

An example of an exploratory walk would be to wade through a gentle stream or to explore a pile of leaves. Run over a fallen tree trunk with your puppy or balance on a wall. Please be careful not to overwhelm him or force him to do something he does not want to. Should your Bernese Mountain Dog be afraid, tease him onto the tree trunk with a treat. It is important, that he makes the decision. Here you can also reward small accomplishments and, in this way, introduce him to new things.

The third part of building a bond is grooming. Even though his thin puppy fur does not need much attention, it is recommended to get your bundle of trouble used to brushing. While he is a puppy, a massage glove is enough to massage his skin and fur. Most Bernese Mountain Dogs love that and it will make grooming a positive experience for him.

From the beginning, get him used to having his fur, eyes, ears, paws and lips checked regularly, a few times a week. I also recommend that you get him used to you cleaning his paws from very early on, if they are dirty. Repeat it for practice purposes, even if it is not necessary.

If your Bernese Mountain Dog protests, continue with your routine without hesitation. Stay calm and ignore his defensive behaviour. After a short while he will tolerate it. Naturally, you can reward him at the end with a treat or his toy.

How to get your puppy housetrained

One of the first things a dog owner wants is for his dog to be housetrained. Unfortunately, this is where a lot of mistakes are made, which can negatively influence the human-dog relationship permanently. You can read below how to avoid that and teach him what is right and what is a "no go".

As already described in a previous chapter, it is necessary to spend a lot of time with your puppy. Keep him close to you and do not let him out of your sight. As soon as he looks as if he needs to relieve himself (usually he will sniff around a lot and turn in circles), it is urgent, that you bring him outside. Normally, you will not have time to call him, by that time the accident has already happened. Grab him and carry him out.

Praise him profusely, if he relieves himself outside. In addition, it is recommended that you make a sound signal when your puppy relieves himself, for example "go on" or "hurry up". This has the advantage that he will associate this signal with his action. This can be very useful for you, particularly if you are in a hurry.

It is useful to know, that puppies react to certain situations by wanting to relieve themselves. In those cases, you can be proactive and, as a precautionary measure, take him outside. That could be, for example, after eating or playing or when he has just woken up. You should take him out as soon as that activity is finished. The less the dog has the possibility to relieve himself in the house, the quicker he will learn that he should only do it outside.

Do not be surprised if your Bernese Mountain Dog sometimes makes a "greeting drop", when he gets excited because of visitors arriving. That is perfectly normal. If you know in advance that guests are coming, you should take him to the place, where he can relieve himself directly before they arrive.

In order to avoid that your little Bernese Mountain Dog has an accident in the night, it is recommended that you let him sleep in a dog box or similar at first. Dogs of all breeds have a problem sleeping where they have had such an accident. Your puppy is no different and he will become restless or even make a sound when he is ready to go out. Once you have achieved that, you have the chance to take him out early enough to prevent accidents. If a puppy needs to go out about every 2 hours during the day, you will see that his rhythm slows down noticeably during the night. Even so, it is possible that you will need to take him out once or twice during the night. Be prepared and have shoes and jacket ready at the door.

The absolute "no go" by training your puppy is to combine scolding with having an accident. Think about what I have often explained before. Your dog is not a human and does not think like a human. He will not understand your punishment or your scolding. If you shout at him for making a puddle in the living room, he will never understand that you are angry because he has done it inside and not outside.

For him the only logical conclusion is: My master is angry because I relieved myself, so I will not do that in his presence anymore. This is something that you never want to permanently ingrain into the subconscious of your puppy.

If an accident happens, it happens and you cannot change it. Neither scolding nor praise is suitable in this case. The accident should be cleared up without reaction from you.

The first commands

Feeding

As explained at the beginning of this chapter, you should refrain from training during the first few weeks. After that, you can start training your puppy in small doses. I recommend, as a starting exercise, the systematic setting up of the feeding routine. This exercise has several advantages: Firstly, it increases the bonding with you, because you are responsible for his **feeding**. Secondly, it decreases the danger, that your Bernese Mountain Dog will defend his food against you and it lays the ground work for the *calling off* command.

It would be best to link this exercise with an indirect rank indication, by always giving your Bernese Mountain Dog his food after the family has had theirs. When it is time for him to eat, do the following:

1. One member of the family holds the puppy a short distance away from his feeding place.
2. In the meantime, you prepare his food. Make sure he notices you are doing that. As soon as you have his attention, he will want to come

to you. This is an ideal prerequisite for the exercise.

3. When his food is ready, kneel down and hold his food bowl in front of you. As soon as you have taken that position, your family member should let the puppy go. When the puppy moves towards you and the bowl, give him the command "here".

4. The puppy storms towards you. As soon as he arrives, praise him, put his bowl down in front of you and let him enjoy his food.

Repeat this exercise each feeding time, which is three to four times a day with puppies. The routine and, most importantly, the timing of the command has great significance.

If your puppy has mastered not only this exercise but also the "sit" command, you should add **waiting in front of the food bowl** to the routine.

To do this, repeat points 1 – 3 above exactly as written. Then continue as follows:

4. The puppy storms towards you. This time you do not praise him but give him the command "sit" as soon as he arrives.

5. Put down the food bowl only after he has obeyed the command.

6. **Important:** The puppy may not eat yet. He must wait a few seconds before you give him the "eat" command.

You should vary the time your puppy has to wait before he is allowed to eat. At the beginning it should only be a few moments. Later, you could do something, like wiping the preparation surfaces, before you let him eat.

If you do this exercise consistently at every meal time, you will achieve a completely different basis for your relationship than most dog owners. I can tell you from my own experience, that most dog owners will ridicule you for this consistency. Some people may even consider it to be cruelty. It is not. Always remember that your Bernese Mountain Dog is not a human. In the pack, the pack leader gives the signal as to whom can eat and when. For him that is normal.

In addition, you will notice how strong your commitment to each other has become and how he now accepts your authority. After that, you will not have the problem that your dog growls if you want to touch his food, because he knows that you have the sovereignty over him.

Sit

Now we come to the exercise - **sit**. This is not only one of the most important exercises, but also one of the easiest.

1. Hold your hand over your puppy's head with a treat in it. He will probably try to take it from you one way or another. You should not allow that. When he jumps up, close your hand and ignore his behaviour. Stay calm and try not to say anything.

2. When your Bernese Mountain Dog becomes too tired to hold his head up, he will sit down to make it easier to look up. As soon as he sits down completely, give him the command "sit" and, at the same, time give him his reward.

You will already notice, after a few days, that your dog will understand this exercise. On average, a dog needs to carry out an exercise successfully at least 100 times for him to internalise it permanently.

It is important with all exercises that they are carried out cleanly. If your Bernese Mountain Dog does not sit down completely, or if he jumps up from the seated position, you must not reward him. Wait a few moments until he sits properly then you can give him his treat.

Sit is a quiet exercise so your voice and your body language should be peaceful.

Sit for advanced training is when you do not stand in front of your little Bernese Mountain Dog but allow him to sit beside you. This is a little more difficult, but you will benefit from this exercise in every day life, for example when you have to stand at the roadside, waiting for traffic or when you receive visitors at home.

In order to practice this, hold the treat at your side. If he masters this exercise, let him sit a bit longer before you give him his reward.

Lie down

The next step in the training is the exercise – **lie down**. You should not start this until your Bernese Mountain Dog has mastered the *sit* exercise and is able to stay in that position for a short period of time. *Lie down* is best practised when your dog is a little tired because then he is happier to lie down than when he is full of energy.

This is how you teach him the *lie down* exercise.

1. Allow your Bernese Mountain Dog to sit.
2. As soon as he is sitting quietly, hold a treat in front of his nose.
3. Lower the treat, making sure that you stay close to the puppy so that he does not jump up.
4. He will try to reach the treat, so he will follow you down into the lying position.
5. As soon as he is lying completely, give him the command "lie down" and give him his reward.

Finish exercise

At the same time, you are practising *lie down*, I recommend you to practise **finish exercise.** What do I mean by that?

As I already mentioned, the pack leader decides what is to be done. That is why we spoke in a previous chapter about not reacting to the play wishes of your Bernese Mountain Dog. Deciding when to stop an activity is equally as important as deciding when to start one. Your Bernese Mountain Dog should learn from the start that only you can decide what happens when. This applies to petting, playing and also training.

This is how you train *finish exercise* as an example with the *sit* exercise.

6. After you have rewarded your Bernese Mountain Dog, let him sit again.
7. Then give him the *finish exercise* command by saying "let's go" and make clear to him with your body language, that he should finish the exercise.

Once you have mastered these basic exercises, you are ready to start with the real training of basic knowledge. You will learn how to do this in the following chapter.

Training basic knowledge

Congratulations!

You have achieved a lot with your little Bernese Mountain Dog once you have reached the *training basic knowledge* stage. You have lain the foundation and you will see, that the rest is not so difficult, as you are a well-coordinated team and your Bernese Mountain Dog knows, who is the boss.

In this chapter you will learn the 7 basics I believe every dog owner and every one of their dogs should know off by heart. So that this works for you, below you will learn how to do this step by step.

Let's do it!

Walking on the Lead

Every dog owner wishes that he had trained his dog consistently to walk well on the lead, but very few are ready to put in the work necessary. This applies particularly to owners of large breeds, to which the Bernese Mountain Dog belongs. In comparison to a 4 lb dog which any child can hold, despite him pulling on the lead, your four-legged friend will develop enormous strength. If this strength is not under control – your control – this could lead to dangerous situations, not only for you and your Bernese Mountain Dog but also for third persons. This is why lead leadership is the most important thing when walking your little Bernese Mountain Dog.

There is another reason why you should never let your dog pull on the lead and in principle it is always the same reason. Only the pack leader decides where the pack is going. If your dog is pulling on the lead and you allow it, that means for your Bernese Mountain Dog, that he is deciding the route. If you continue to allow him to gain the authority it is unclear to him why he should take notice of you in other things. You can see that this is a recurring theme throughout the training.

In addition to the above, the operant conditioning already mentioned in this book will ensure that when your puppy is successful in pulling you, you allow him to be the leader, so he will continue to do it. Once he has linked that together, it will be very difficult for you to change his behaviour. Particularly by Bernese Mountain Dogs, these links are often forged much quicker than their owners would like. Always remember the operant conditioning works in both positive and negative senses.

I would suggest: Please take your lead leadership seriously. You could improve the image of the Bernese Mountain Dog sustainably when people see that your dog does not pull on the lead. You will discover below how to do this:

1. Walk with your puppy on the lead. If he sees something interesting, he will start to pull in a particular direction.
2. Stand still immediately and do not react. Do not speak to your Bernese Mountain Dog, just wait.
3. Your Bernese Mountain Dog may not react immediately, but after a while he will change

his behaviour. Perhaps he will sit down or come running to you. You should continue walking only after he has loosened the tension on the lead.

4. When he has loosened the tension, give him the command "slowly". If you repeat this often enough, he will link the action with the command.

5. Important: As soon as he starts to pull again, stand reactionless until the lead loses tension again.

You need a lot of patience for this exercise. Your little Bernese Mountain Dog will often pull on the lead, at the beginning as soon as he sees, smells or hears something interesting. It is up to you to ensure, that when the tension increases, you react immediately. The work you invest in this will be rewarded for the rest of your dog's life. There is nothing more pleasant, than a relaxed walk with your dog, without having to fight for control.

Walking to heel

Once your Bernese Mountain Dog has learned to walk on the lead, the next step is to master the command "heel". What is the difference between lead leadership and "heel"? While you are practising lead leadership, the goal is that your dog does not pull on the lead. "Heel" is much more. This is when your Bernese Mountain Dog pays attention to you all the time and walks next to you with a loose lead at all times. It makes no difference whether you turn a corner, stand still or step over an obstacle, your dog will stay in step with you.

As puppies and young dogs generally cannot go for any length of time to *heel*, good lead leadership is very important.

However, before you begin to practice this new command, you should decide which side your dog should walk on. It is not recommended to keep changing sides, it is better to be consistent.

It is up to you, which side you choose. I personally prefer the left side. Why? Because of the traffic. If you are often walking along busy roads, that could be useful. Even the best-trained dog can scare on hearing sudden noises and could do something unexpectedly. If he is walking on your right, this could mean that he inadvertently pushes you and you both end up in the road. I do not need to describe here what that can mean. That said, it is only my personal opinion, there is no specific "better" side.

If you should also decide on the left side you should have his treats in your left jacket pocket. You hold the lead with the right hand. If you decide on the right side, just do the opposite.

This is how you start training:

1. To ensure that your Bernese Mountain Dog stays at your side, you should keep his attention on you. You can do this best with treats. Entice your Bernese Mountain Dog to the side you want him to walk on.
2. As soon as he directs his full attention to the treat, start walking determinedly and quickly. Give the command "heel".
3. While you are walking, continue occasionally to say the command.

4. After a short while (after a few meters with puppies), let him sit and give him the treat as his reward.

During the whole exercise it is acceptable if your puppy tries to lick or nibble the treat. One thing he should not do is to jump up. Choose the distance for this exercise based on the span of his attention. At the beginning this will be very short and you should not overdo it.

If you are able to do this exercise without problems, you can try to do it without the treat. At the beginning, it is recommended to keep your hand in your pocket where the treats are but, after a while, you can let your arm hang down. If your Bernese Mountain Dog is walking attentively by your side, reward him with a treat. Slowly you should extend the time between rewards.

The following points should also be noted:

- Vary your route and do not just walk straight ahead. Walk in curves or sometimes backwards. Walk quicker or slower. You could perhaps run down a flight of stairs or step over a tree trunk. Your Bernese

Mountain Dog should stay at your side at all times during these variations.

- As soon as you notice that your puppy has become distracted, motivate him by speaking with an excited voice. The rest of the time it is recommended to say as little as possible, so that his attention is not diluted. Should your little friend stand still or try to go in a different direction, ignore his behaviour and continue walking at a good pace. As soon as he directs his full attention towards you and walks beside you, praise him.

- If your Bernese Mountain Dog continues to sniff around or to walk too quickly, walk in tight circles with him being on the inside. In this way, you obstruct his path and prevent him from sniffing. Here too, as soon as he directs his full attention towards you, you should praise him.

Calling your dog

We already laid the foundation for calling your dog in the previous chapter about feeding. You remember, that your Bernese Mountain Dog is held by a second person while you prepare his food. As soon as you are in position with his bowl, as he is freed and runs towards you, you give him the command "here".

If your dog responds by running towards his food without a problem, you can increase the difficulty of the exercise a little. Now you can start to call him in-between feeding times and without him being held by another person. Before you start, you should ensure that he will not be distracted, or was just sleeping. Attract his attention to you with excitement in your voice. Give the command "here" while he is already on his way to you.

If you can master this exercise within your own four walls without difficulties, you can try it outside. Ideally, this would be on your balcony or in your garden. If this works well over a longer period of time, you can increase the difficulty a second time by leaving the garden.

I have a few **secret tips** for you to ensure that the *calling* exercise really works.

- Practice the *calling* command at least three weeks each in your house, in your own garden or balcony and ensure that there are no distractions. The success your puppy experiences during this time will be engrained firmly in his subconscious.

- Ensure, that you draw your dog's attention with an excited voice, before you call him. Only give the command "here" when you are sure that he is coming to you and is relatively close to you. After that you can increase the distance in stages.

- In order to increase his wish to come to you, you can systematically move further away from him, when you draw his attention.

- Ensure that your Bernese Mountain Dog is hungry when you train this technique, particularly when you are away from the house or garden. Should he feel a little hunger, he will be particularly keen to react to a treat.

If you follow these tips and systematically build up the exercise, you will experience a lot of success: Your Bernese Mountain Dog will come directly to you, when you call him without you having to offer him treats.

Once you have mastered this exercise, you should start to prepare distractions for him. This could be playing children, other dogs or an interesting smell. Despite all these distractions, your little four-legged friend should come to you immediately when you call him. It is particularly useful to use your puppy's hunger to your advantage, when teaching this exercise.

At the beginning of the exercise, it is not yet necessary to make your dog sit after he has come to you. This would lead to your puppy thinking that the treat is connected to the *sit* command and not to the *calling*. As soon as the training is going well and you are experiencing some success, you can start to use the *sit* command, after the Bernese Mountain Dog has received his treat. After countless repeats and preferably not starting until your Bernese Mountain Dog is no longer a puppy, you can let him sit before he receives his treat.

<u>Stay</u>

Once your Bernese Mountain Dog has mastered the *stay* exercise, you will notice that everyday life with him is easier and more relaxed. You may be asking yourself why, as many dog owners do not see any value in this exercise. The answer is simple: If you have taught your dog to wait patiently for you, you could let him out of your sight for a few moments without being afraid, that he will run away or get up to mischief. This is helpful when he returns from a walk covered in dirt and you allow him to sit quietly at the front door while you get a towel. Or he could sit outside the pharmacist, while you are inside buying something.

This is how you train the *stay* command:

1. Allow your Bernese Mountain Dog to "sit" or "lie down" next to you
2. Once he is sitting or lying, relaxed, you say "stay" and stand directly in front of him. At the beginning, just stay in front of him for a few moments. Hold the lead in your hand during this exercise to correct any bad behaviour that might occur. Ensure that the lead is not tight.

3. Go and stand beside him again and praise him.

Once you can do this exercise without mistakes, increase the difficulty. You can do that by increasing the time you stand in front of your Bernese Mountain Dog. If he can stay at least one minute, quietly sitting, you can raise the difficulty again. Now you can go a few meters away from him, at first only for a short time, then for longer. If he manages to sit quietly and relaxed for at least 2 minutes at the full length of his lead, you have mastered the first milestone.

Your dog is now able to sit where he is told to without being distracted. To add another degree of difficulty, you can add a small amount of distraction to the exercise. You do not stand still in front of him but walk parallel to your Bernese Mountain Dog, up and down. Not for long, at first, and not far away. After a while, you can increase both distance and length of time.

If he is able to carry out this exercise, you can walk in semicircles and eventually in full circles around him. Once this does not cause him any problems, you can go onto the big challenge: Go out of his range of view for a short time. I recommend you give him the *lie down* command before you do that. Particularly with this exercise, I would recommend that you start with very short periods of time and distances, which you can increase as time goes by.

Here are a few **secret tips** to master the exercise even better:

- The exercises "stay" and "sit" are quiet training times. Your body language and voice should therefore be peaceful.
- To make it easier for your Bernese Mountain Dog to wait for you, it is a good idea to tire him out first. If he is full of energy, it is difficult for him to stay in one place or in the same position.
- Do not start this exercise until your dog can lie, relaxed, beside you for least 2 minutes.
- At the beginning, always train on the lead with him, but let it hang loosely, as described above. If your Bernese Mountain Dog stands up during the exercise, it is probable that the time was too long or the distance too great. Take him back to the exact place, that he was sitting or lying, and repeat the exercise from the beginning.

- Remember, the exercise is not finished until you are standing next to your Bernese Mountain Dog again. Allow him to sit up before you give him his reward. This detail is particularly important with the exercise *lie down* because your dog will be tense during the exercise. Once he knows that he must lie until you are standing next to him, he can relax a little.

- Carry out this exercise for a few weeks in the *sit* position after which you can sometimes call him to you from the *stay* position.

- Be aware of the timing of the reward. Do not hold a treat in the hand all the time because your puppy will find it even more difficult to wait for the calling command. It will be even more difficult for him, if you take the treat out of your pocket while you are walking towards him. Wait until you are standing beside him. Often, it is enough just to praise your dog after the exercise.

Sit at a distance

At first, many people think that "sit at a distance" is the same as the exercise "stay" while sitting. However, it is not the same. *Sit at a distance* is the highest level of difficulty with respect to the classical *sit* command. This exercise is particularly helpful if you and your Bernese Mountain Dog suddenly have to stop and it is important that he is able to remain in a particular place, as soon as you give the command, even if you are not with him.

For example, it is possible that a jogger or bike rider suddenly appears and your Bernese Mountain Dog has gone a little ahead of you; or he has to cross over a street when you call him. In these situations, you can avoid danger, if your Bernese Mountain Dog sits and obediently waits for you. This is really an advanced exercise, however, and should not be trained at puppy age. I wanted to tell you about it anyway because I think it is very important to know.

This is how you build up your exercise systematically:

1. When you use the command "sit", stretch your arm outwards and upwards as a *listen* signal.

2. As soon as you think your dog has linked the combination of voice and arm, practice using the command only with the arm. If your Bernese Mountain Dog sits down competently when commanded, you can start to increase the distance.

3. If your four-legged friend finds himself a few meters away from you, without any distractions, draw his attention towards you. As soon as he stops and looks at you, give him the arm signal. After he has sat down, walk slowly towards him and reward him.

4. Once this exercise is carried out competently, you can increase the distance.

5. If the exercise is also successful at a distance, start training the exercise again at shorter distances, this time with distractions. Once he is competent with this exercise, despite distractions, you can increase the distance a little at a time.

When you have mastered this exercise, you will not only have the benefit that your dog will sit at a distance, but also you will experience, that your dog will look much more in your direction and want to make eye contact. You will notice an increase in the strength of your bond with your dog.

Giving something up

Many dog owners connect the command "leave" with scolding for bad behaviour by their dog. As with previous exercises, the real intention of this command is to invoke a particular behavioural pattern from your puppy. Examples of this are, if you want your Bernese Mountain Dog to drop a toy or slipper or even a bone, which he has in his mouth.

It is obvious to most why this command is useful in everyday life. However, it is particularly important to me, that this exercise is not connected with fear, but that your dog will learn, through consistency, targeted training and well-timed reward.

You will find out how to do it following the steps below:

1. Your Bernese Mountain Dog is holding something in his mouth, that he is not supposed to.
2. Instead of shouting at him, lure him towards you using an excited voice.
3. As soon as he reaches you, offer him an exchange. This could either be his favourite toy or a treat.

4. Once he has dropped the item, give him the command "leave".

5. Repeat this exercise as often as you can. Soon he will let the item go, when you give the command, without you having to offer him something.

Another, longer method is to say "leave" every time your puppy drops something by himself. This demands a lot of attention from you, because you must really do it every time.

You should never make this mistake: Never run after your dog, when he is supposed to drop something. Running after him would cause your Bernese Mountain Dog to associate, that he has to hide his prey from you, which would make it even more difficult to break this habit. Apart from that, the little guy is much quicker and more agile than you are.

Putting the lead on and taking it off

Putting the lead on and taking it off is another example of an exercise, which is completely neglected by most dog owners. They do not see any sense or added value in building up a systematic routine for this. At the same time, they become angry when their dogs become impatient and do not want their leads taken off or put it on.

If you want to avoid this from happening, you should get your puppy used to the following routine from the beginning, whenever you take his lead off.

1. Use the command *sit* every time you want to put on or take off his lead.
2. Once you have taken his lead off or put it on, let him sit in front of you for a few moments.
3. Wait until he is quiet and, ideally, makes eye contact with you.
4. Only then you should allow him to go, using the command "go on".

The main point of this exercise is to make your Bernese Mountain Dog wait quietly and to gain his attention. If his attention wanders and he pulls away from you before you give the command, you are rewarding the wrong behaviour. You already know, without me telling you, what the consequences are of allowing this link to form in his subconscious.

My tip: Hold your little friend inconspicuously by the collar when you take off his lead. If he wants to escape before you allow it, you can immediately slow him down and hold him back. Avoid at all costs, providing him with an undesirable sense of achievement.

Conclusion

Congratulations!

You have taken the first step, one which not every dog owner is prepared to do. You have informed yourself comprehensively about the training of your Bernese Mountain Dog and will be able to build a much more contented and relaxed relationship with your four-legged friend than most people.

This is because you know what is most important:

- You know the difference between humans and dogs as pack animals. You will not be intimidated, when acquaintances laugh at you, only because your dog has to wait for his food, because you know why you are doing it.

- You have taken to heart the importance of consistency in the training of your dog. That is, why you take care with everything you do and question his behaviour continually. You know, that mistakes creep in, slowly and quietly, without you noticing and you want to avoid that.

- You know, that many things, which seem unimportant to humans, could have an indirect consequence to your puppy's ranking in the family. This includes the order of eating; who is allowed to go where and who decides where to go. You use this knowledge to keep constant and safe control over your puppy and he needs to know that, to become a confident, relaxed and contented dog.

- You know about both operant and classical conditioning and know how to use them when training your Bernese Mountain Dog. You know which role, both negative and positive, this training has on your dog, so you are able to prevent him from gaining a sense of achievement for something you do not want him to do.

- You know how to train basic elements with your puppy in easy stages. You know, that it is not enough only to expect obedience sometimes and not others and you know how this training will benefit both of you.

- You know, that training puppies has nothing to do with brutal enforcement but is a product of commitment to systematic exercises, good training, countless repeats and loads of patience.

- You know, that the many rules your Bernese Mountain Dog has to learn, will not harm him but, on the contrary, will help him to understand your world. You give him a home, which he can see as his pack and ensure systematic routines and pecking orders, which he needs. You give him security and leadership.

- Through consistent and loving care for your Bernese Mountain Dog, you will ensure a relaxed everyday life and you will benefit by achieving an intensive and intimate relationship with him. You will see, that people who ridicule your methods, will be envious of your well-brought up dog.

Lastly, I have one more tip for you:

Read this book more than once. It would be best to read it several times before your Bernese Mountain Dog moves in. While you are beginning your training, it will not harm to refer to this book from time to time.

I wish you and your puppy every imaginable success for your future. Above all, I wish you harmony, love and many years together.

Yours
Claudia

Did you enjoy my book?

Now you have read my book, you know how best to train your little Bernese Mountain Dog puppy. This is why I am asking you now for a small favour. Customer reviews are an important part of every product offered by Amazon. It is the first thing that customers look at and, more often than not, is the main reason whether or not they decide to buy the product. Considering the endless number of products available at Amazon, this factor is becoming increasingly important.

If you liked my book, I would be more than grateful if you could leave your review by Amazon. How do you do that? Just click on the "Write a customer review"-button (as shown below), which you find on the Amazon product page of my book or your orders site:

Review this product

Share your thoughts with other customers

Write a customer review

Just write a short review as to whether you particularly liked my book or if there is something I can improve on. It will not take more than 2 minutes, honestly!

Be assured, I will read every review personally. It will help me a lot to improve my books and to tailor them to your wishes.

For this I say to you:

Thank you very much!

Yours

Claudia

References:

Schlegl-Kofler, Katharina: Unser Welpe. 3rd edition. Munich: Published 2009 by GRÄFE UND UNZER

Schlegl-Kofler, Katharina: Hunde-erziehung. 3rd edition. Munich: Published 2009 by GRÄFE UND UNZER

Niewöhner, Imken: Auf ins Leben!: Grundschulplan für Welpen. 1st edition. Nerdlen: Published 2012 by Kynos

Rätke, Jana; Perfahl, Barbara: Abenteuer Welpe. 1st edition. Nerdlen: Published 2017 by Kynos

Millan, Cesar; Peltier, Melissa Jo: Tipps vom Hundeflüsterer: Einfache Maßnahmen für die gelungene Beziehung zwischen Mensch und Hund. 1st edition. Munich: Published 2009 by Arkana

Koring, Mel: Welpenschule: Das 8-Wochen-Training. 1st edition. Stuttgart: Published 2018 by Kosmos

Winkler, Sabine: So lernt mein Hund: Der Schlüssel für die erfolgreiche Erziehung und Ausbildung. 3rd edition. Stuttgart: Published by Kosmos

Bürner, Margit; Bürner, Evi: Berner Sennenhund: Auswahl, Haltung, Erziehung, Beschäftigung. 1. Auflage. Stuttgart: Kosmos Verlag 2010

Schneider-Weissbaum, Anita: Berner Sennenhund. 1. Auflage. Stuttgart: Müller Rüschlikon 2012

Disclaimer